I JUST SAID

FORGET
THIS GOOD THING
I JUST SAID

Aphorisms 2018-2021

By Colin Dodds

Layout by Rachel Greene for eflinpen designs

Cover by Adam Lewin

ISBN: 978-0-578-95150-8

It's hard, at first, to spot the shimmer that becomes your life

*

My daughter says her dreams always start in the middle, like how the year begins on a Wednesday in the middle of a pay period in winter

*

I will try not to abuse the privilege of your attention

My wife puts away Christmas tree ornaments with a tenderness that proves something no calamity can disprove

*

The outcome is always necessarily in doubt

*

I've sung and suffered, hidden in thickets of whisper treaties and climbed salmon ladders of degradation. I fear the time is near when I must speak plainly or die dishonest

Hurry up and tell the story
before poetry can suf-
focate it

*

I told my little girl about
death. She asked if I was
joking. I said *no*, and she
said *I wish it was a joke*

*

There is a return. We know
this as surely as the maze
confounds us

Every morning someone decides *no more*. But not me. I have mouths to feed and mouths to shut the fuck up

*

One question before we start: Do we want to get it more right or more wrong?

*

If it's real fear, you may not know until years after it lifts. It will have seemed like sound reasoning in the best of all possible worlds

Why is it two o'clock? my daughter asks. Oh, how I sputter

*

The glittering skyline is made of failure and dirt

*

Try to avoid an adventure, and misadventure rears up

The glittering skyline is propaganda. You can feel your own salesy effort when you try to appreciate it

*

My agenda? I'm like that victim on the news—critical but stable

*

Reality is a fountain

Gangrene sets in quickly. Blessed nature is a billion-faced, poorly raised son of a bitch asking *Hey, you eating that?*

*

There's never been a sky so blue as to know no vultures

*

Reserve the right to be rather unreasonable

Hey, you eating that? again
and again like the trill of the
cicada horde

*

One of the great curses laid
upon humanity is the abject
inability to tell a blessing
from a curse

*

There's a fire. Everyone
crowds the door to matter

Under pressure with no plan—so comes G-d or disaster, in famously unequal measure

*

Why is absolutely everything still under consideration? I thought it was late

*

I keep asking, though the answer is often: *Because fuck you*

Listen for the song sung
with air that wants no song
sung into air that wants no
song sung

*

If you're breaking a
promise you never made,
at least you're not making a
promise you can't keep

*

Look at your hands, front
and back. They're a symbol
beyond language, re-
minding

Staring down the possibility of a dead son in my wife's belly through the long ride to the hospital, G-d seems to say *Smarten up. Your ideas are not good enough*

*

Hurry up. Tell it before the devil knows your drink, before the president knows your name

*

G-d's favor or disfavor often speaks to me through a woman's body

Tired, I'll agree we all need
a story like a bird needs a
nest or a fox needs a
burrow

*

Like a tightrope walker
don't look down. Like a
magician don't say how

*

I try to feel the way
someone else looks. But
they catch me, and try it
back

How I look is not how I feel
is not what I'm for

                    *

I hold my breath to hold a
thought. I say *eyes eyes*
just to watch

                    *

Something matters. For us
lacking   subtlety,   death
seems a clue

A pigeon or a dozen eggs intercept me at my doorstep to remind me I haven't been forgotten

*

Having not forsaken the ill-worn proposition of my own specialness, I locate an unsurveilled grove and try to claim the full privilege and price of a human being

*

Be dazzled and aroused. Recall the belonging to which you were invited by a fleeting image

Sometimes you don't know
what you think until you
start talking

*

Something older than
childhood beckons—the
calendar stone of Boston,
the soap that blinks with
the faces of the ancient
unborn

*

Snakes own the diamond
mine where men go to get
rich. The men spend their
wages on food to replace
the blood the snakes drink

No sooner had mankind
had its first idea than it had
the wrong idea

*

Pursuing a chirp heard
before I hatched, I wander
the earth

*

Some days are a highwire
made of burning bullshit,
spun by no one so trust-
worthy as a spider

It may never be as hard as this ever again. And when it's over, I'll miss it terribly

*

The tyrant-parasite and the true savior eventually come to an uneasy accommodation—something only a catastrophically broken heart could broker

*

I play nice all day with baby. But G-d comes at night, and He wants a rematch

Little nothings of light ripple along the crippled turnpike on the morning of the taxi strike

*

He fell off the highwire and now he's somebody's dad. He fell off the highwire and now he's the fault line in somebody's heart

*

All I ever saw of the unborn one was a butterfly of brown blood on the sheets

Today was before, and will
resume as a moonbeam in
a sweat bead, a wink from
the smear trail of the street
sweeper in diagonal morn-
ing light

*

My dead friend and I say
*I'm tired. I'll see you
tomorrow*, both knowing
we're lying, but lying
anyway

*

The inexhaustible promise
of morning defeats me for
breakfast

New York Harbor lights up
at dusk. And I want to say
*so sorry you didn't get to
see it.* Then the fluorescent
lights spring on to say *no
one does, not really*

*

One day, the cliff face will
release the drill marks of
the dynamite that exposed
it to the highway

*

You get to choose, or not
choose, if you decide

A dream, a song—then off
to the maelstrom of weird
abuses, to the shit we have
to eat to even be alive

*

Things that should matter
forever vanish in a murky
backwash of minutiae.
Even the devil helps the
aggrieved, sometimes

*

The sun throws us to and
fro more than we can
summon the intellect to
imagine

I was tutored in New York
scripture, dense and
treacherous

*

Welcome say the Janus-
faced vaginas of the
Brooklyn Bridge

*

Every airy fantasy is woven
on a loom of violence

Red-bottomed boats in the harbor ignore the glossy office aquarium towers of momentarily necessary monsters

*

The hardest way to keep your balance is to stand still

*

You're working a bad job. And I'm here for a drug that helps me work a slightly less bad job. That's better than a lie, right?

The avenue at rush hour is
full of predation dressed as
pleasure and vice versa.
Survival and entertainment
are the least of what is
happening

*

They think about the
ingredients of the lan-
gostino salad and the price
of palladium. They don't
think about you

*

An octagonal bucket
connects the Hugh Carey
Tunnel to the pearlescent
empyrean, offering up
black traffic mist to a
hungry nostril

The bowl of the horizon
curves like the shins of a
newborn

*

Perhaps for G-d to say one
coherent thing to you, He'd
need to begin speaking six
thousand years ago

*

The shrapnel of forgotten
wars still fly in the necktie,
the glare of a windshield,
and the half-laugh at the
misheard word

Nature is a gargantuan
snooze. But you'll lose your
mind if you don't sleep

*

Like time and space, I'm a
dubious interlocutor

*

So much love, desperation,
work and deep joy goes
into one more spiritual
false start

So much love, desperation, work, and deep joy goes into becoming more junk on a screen

*

We hear *bless you* two, three times. Only later do we hear the sneezes

*

On stylish streets, people sharpen the syntax of what they mean, only to give away their real life stories by accident

Death is a grand tradition,
like pursuing what you
don't honestly desire

*

*A solar-powered grave-
yard*, she said. I never
found out if it was a
damning verdict or an
exciting business plan

*

Depends on whether or not
I see my shadow. Hate that
guy

Daily responsibilities are
trauma enough at a certain
pitch of consciousness

*

The goblins of exile grind
out typos all day long

*

The gimmick and the ruin
can stand still. My eyes
dance like bees

Metaphors cross con-
taminate. Words form the
mouth

*

At the end, we discover the
apocalypse was an over-
ture, with every over-
stylized villain we'd later
become already present at
the original divorce

*

The story that makes the
entire continent of reality
into an obstacle. It presses
through every friend

Going to and fro across the earth, rolling and tumbling and crying, I was crowned like a street or like a shit, given a form that's hard to accept

*

Into a drama of rental cars and adulterous near misses, a crack of lightning split the cosmos in New Hampshire

*

Poets climb the mountain of purgatory by night

That I was a flicker in a void, making up stories; That my vocabulary was incomplete, and so I was free to speak. Who would tell me these things?

*

It's a bootstrap operation. You do it from despair, on faith

*

Work is a kind of sleep—a quarter dream, half of one discomfort

A glimpse of men wrestling
chickens into gray plastic
garbage cans at the
slaughterhouse to start
each morning has a
stabilizing effect on the
mind

*

The average person heard
what you were saying
about him, and he's pissed

*

There's a pungent irony
when you argue on behalf
of a fuller reality

There are dead spots in the facade. Not every creditor will even break a nose. The biggest bullies rely on ribbons and bows

*

Wealth is poison and poverty kills

*

Peasants muster by the tits of reality—ever so full of strategies!

Because the airport appears real and I am ever in doubt

*

To the dumpster, to the throne—we were all chased from somewhere

*

Assholes walked in acting like customers, saying *we're being helped*, as if they could be

Some speech is more than
free. It costs the listener

*

Success has a thousand
fathers. Failure is an
orphan. The day is the
bastard son of a thousand
maniacs

*

Some folks say you get
what you get. But that gets
to be bullshit, too

Wealth immolates into a million ineffectual devotions to calisthenics, aesthetics and anesthetics

*

I said I slipped, but that was a lie. I threw the fight, sold out to peripheral interests for the proverbial short money

*

We eat out every night. Side dishes hem in our cosmos

There is little trust and
everyone works as some
form of babysitter

*

Each new invention is a
wearisome thing, de-
manding *Redeem This!*

*

The gift shops are full of
halos and the delis are full
of sins. It's a grand time to
be flat, flat broke

If we keep on striving, the ornate shadows of star-vation are all we'll ever know

*

No one wants anything within a mile of whatever the fuck you're about? Take solace!

*

This is what the future looks like when the future doesn't come again and again

Summer comes. Suddenly
everyone has the same
secret

*

You can see your reflection
in a grimy, faded orange
traffic cone. But don't

*

The scavengers are brave
and prettier than you might
expect. To doom, they say
yeah I see you seeing me

During the time when you
might think anything at all,
every shadow might house
an eye or a successor

*

The gaze of strangers will
nourish and trouble you.
But you can't starve
untroubled, either

*

Rotund pudendas of shield
faces, bandoliers of egg
and dart: The transmission
tower of reality is usually a
little ridiculous

The withdrawal of religion
feels like the withdrawal of
a hormone

*

*Serial killers and serial
numbers and spree killers,
shopping sprees, mass
killers and critical mass*—it
sure sings like a square
dance

*

The ritual—once called a
human being—obsolesces

Five hundred portents, each one a helicopter, saying *watch your step*

*

How we conspire in the everlasting fire!

*

The first thing that ties you to the ever-foundering age is a riff, a dimple, a trifle. The second is usually a betrayal

Everyone and everything is trying to be cool, my girl explains

*

What does the deli look like after five thousand years?

*

A shadow—contagious as a yawn or rising prices—squats on our brains like a goblin

The spots where sex intersects with religion intersects with politics are uneasy on the eye. Minerva's nipple peeks from the rim of her shield— deadly!

*

Let's talk recreation

*

I checked my phone for the weather, and found every fifteen minutes of fame— yours, mine, the Babylonian Empire's—made wildly interchangeable

When something doesn't feel quite right, don't spend every last cent on it

*

Entertainment shifts to a straight analgesic. We argue over the daydreams we can be trusted with, and prove we can be trusted with precious fucking little

*

World Wide Whip—wield it or have it wielded upon you

I was there when the money was spent—every dollar an arthritic knot in a back-twisting labor or mind-bending sleight—sent to oblivion with glee!

*

There's a new blurriness to the present—a draft from fore and aft

*

One of us is an asshole. We're trying to get through the night without finding out who

I am no longer a cool spirit
flitting among quaint and
curious volumes of for-
gotten lore, but a consumer
of broadband. They say I
agreed to it

*

The time to pretend it is
another time has run out

*

Maybe I've lost my mind, or
maybe I just feel the teeth
of the tick that's drinking
my blood

Memories blur to echoes of action figures of reveries of pictures of anecdotes of movies... The copier gets sloppier

*

Inside a gigantic book that reads itself, why do or say anything?

*

I lose such chunks of my humanity arguing with fools who don't exist

A new tower ten miles off
pokes through the avenue's
treetops. Built as sold, it's
tall, and that's all

*

An engine holds up the
walls, and a pill lets them
drift

*

The crisis tightens its grip,
but loses its force. The tip
of the breaking wave
seems to boil as it grows
thin

Beside the great salt lick of real, verified existence, love was never going to be enough

*

The wake of the boat looks the same as the inside of a fish

*

The hero wears his medals to bed. The film director insists every naked soul at the orgy learns his name

You see yourself like you see the strangers in the airport—benefited by one too many showers and a pre-owned sense of self-regard

*

Total responsibility seizes some folks until they marvel that a butterfly might flutter past a thornbush and not apologize for being a butterfly

You can acquire boundless
admiration behind a mask,
but to harvest a single drop
of love, you must remove it

*

My meal is more markup
than food, paid for in my
own markup, folded into
someone else's markup.
What could go wrong?

*

There's the cat and what
you choose to ignore about
the cat. Together, they
make a cat—hopefully one
you like, and feed

For those who demand the judgment of G-d, there are slot machines

*

I still get mail in the addled, unmopped places where they saddle angels with human faces

*

The jogger and the insulated window are still poor symbols. But just wait

In the beachhead and graveyard of dreams, the rents never go down

*

I spend a short walk trying to explain verse and chorus to my daughter—the mirth at becoming dismayed, and the delight coming back

*

Who wants to go the distance just to see what the judges say?

There's a valley where, at night, the unicorns turn to vampires

*

The receptionist said the messenger had nice teeth. For us, this was reason to be afraid. But the elders saw it as the weakness it was

*

The devil is without inner reflection, completely reflective in appearance, like a modern office building. Contract-employee demons line its gut

They call it *time*, and we're
supposed to think it's not
thirsty for our warm blood

*

Sleep is the penultimate
mother

*

Man named the animals,
but G-d numbered the days

The radio plays another
song about a man who
wants to do good, but just
can't take it another
second

*

All the damage bore the
signature of builders

*

I climbed Gold Flamingo
Hill to the casino-hospital,
and searched for the right
bartender to overtip to see
a doctor

What some folks call *culture* feels like a gloved hand rubbing uncooked chicken on the pursed lips of infants

*

I punched the mortal timeclock, but my astral penis was at the store

*

You go gunning for the devil, but what gets you is some dumb kid, some trivial habit, some spot blind enough to pass for G-d

Let's resample that well-recorded decade for another millennium. Every kingdom becomes a kingdom of frantic repetition

*

Bodies and souls; angels and devils—each believes they're conning the other. It's what cosmology comes to in an age of media

*

The hopeless cases will fight to stay in hell

Oppressed by the sat-
isfactory, I wear a
prisoner's spit-proof hood
curated by the world's
finest chefs

*

These things we thought
common as water are
gone. A bar week is sixteen
shifts—*that's sixteen shifts
gone*. I'd mourn, but them I
drink with are longer gone

*

It was never much to look
at, but it was a place a
person never entirely
leaves

Screaming serves a couple
purposes. It slows the
breath, which wants no
part of the mess you're in,
and which you're going to
need

*

Dreams renegotiate the
borders and treaties
between ourselves and skin
cancer and steel, corn flour,
our grandmothers and
Jupiter

*

You're a dream, too. You
just happen to be a well-fed
one

The Lower East Side was a jamboree of survival. A lot of people got hurt in ways that would take generations to unwind

*

Intellectual honesty doesn't care what I want. The humanity I smudge from another also comes out of my own account

*

Any ad buyer or copywriter will tell you, there are no heroes in media

A certain tide pounds the jetties of sleep

*

Engraved in the locket of my heart are the perpetually unimpressed expressions of women who grew up too poor to be afraid

*

My daughter has a keen eye for the unhappy actions buzzing all around her. So I teach her history, one treason at a time

Some folks say reality isn't so much a fountain as a toilet in need of flushing

*

Michael O'Momps leads the gang in a lengthy chat about what their last names were supposed to have been

*

People at the funeral are dressed for when they had different bodies

If you can keep alone in it,
a crowd can be nice—a
current against the bait

*

Between the G-d you trust
in and the one you'll admit
to, mind the gap

*

I'm also from a lesser
American city that carefully
pines for the bad old days
when it was better loved

I'm also from a lesser American city in its one hundredth second act— pleading to be plowed by plastic suitcase wheels

*

An archipelago of ship-wreck realities is where you must begin

*

Never marry a corpse, no matter how accomplished

The last guy selling lingerie on Orchard Street will tell you: *The worst thing about success is that it does exist, somewhere else*

*

Born again? I'm still digging out from the first one

*

I'm also from a lesser American city stranded in interest rates and over-sized televisions where lazy-minded faces argue who's owed a Super Bowl

The horizon is marked by the stamp of whoever could keep a straight face that century

*

Who will add a warble to the cold chirp of culture?

*

In the act of dying, what new will there be to see?

Beyond the bosses who torment in service to electricity and water, there's a wilderness that's deaf to us whenever we pause from killing for even a moment

*

Name for me the rivers that separate compulsion from habit from hobby from economic necessity

*

It's hard to know who to root for here in America

Tonight is rooftop drinks.
Tomorrow morning is
airport lines and *you must
be at least this fucked to
ride the ride*

*

G-d is a bandage on a
wound so large as to
beggar imagination and
bankrupt belief

*

No matter how damned
you may be, spurn the
automated blessings

People on rooftops, maybe
ugly and maybe crippled,
kiss

*

Like every light, you fled to
the bushel

*

Quarter to five in the
morning, the birds and
church bells are horny and
loud

There's a troll who'll fix your crystal pony if you bring him the fingers and toes of your peers. You start with the bad kids, but soon run out

*

Big city, big jobs—all fun and games, but to bang your chin on the parallel bars is death itself

*

The cameras get too good, and we all must pay

Nine feet high, the graveside flowers formed a vodka bottle

*

The mote in my eye is a million years old. It's killed millions and sustained millions more

*

Lovely, ugly New York may yet forge its charter to the crackling dawn of time

Ever-busy, the dusty urethras and linty cunts of the non-apocalypse will always water down the booze and say, *don't you mean to say...*

*

Entertainers never give a straight answer. And the entertained have the look of well-corralled prey

*

Solutions metastasize to disasters faster than they did last year

Get Well Fast the card
read. The face of a clock
decorated its front

*

I'm not the first or the last
guy to try hiding under the
devil's feet

*

Make a habit of living at
close quarters with them
who mean you harm, and
soon you can't live without
them

The witches have reasons:
candy or bone marrow or
because the museum
misspent its patrimony. But
at night they turn the
townfolk into statues

*

Luxury luxuriously enforces
itself with the nondescript
music of a waiter gently
collecting the check and
clearing out a dangerous
customer

*

I don't always love how I'm
treated. But I get it

The upscale mall is an airport for the luxuries we would be

*

After everything, people still wave at boats

*

I am subject of the realm, subject to the whim of more than I care to admit

The light is influenced by
lady-sneezes that pile
every consonant against
half a vowel, by the way an
obscure fabric falls across
a belly or buttock

*

Beside the thousand-dollar
belts, a security guard
explains to a diagonal-
faced junkie couple that
they will have to leave

*

*Birthday, Champion, Pre-
sident*—the jive to make
each year seem different
starts to feel desperate

A civilization in which no one ever turns down the money is a sad wet fart

*

Among the well, one must act as if one belongs

*

In the company cafeteria, a colleague warns about a plague of madness among the middle-aged

G-d is not vain. He will show up wearing hand-me-downs, even yours

*

Even a spaceship is boring if you're paying for it

*

The melody's in custody. The sailboat and helicopter deliver time up for execution

I bang my damned shin on another grim, pink-granite extrusion of a civilization gathering up the nerve to say *okay this isn't fun anymore*

*

In full view of the rain, a fountain bursts and burbles

*

Unhappy are the estuaries where the stories we tell about ourselves mingle with the stories we tell about others

The yachts are laced with lights and spaced like a valedictorian's knees. Obnoxious beauty pouts in obvious cages. The atrium is a turbine of mis-understood energy

*

The day is like a shrapnel ricochet—its source and trajectory obscure and frightening

*

The glass-sheathed col-ossus is willfully invisible, like a father hissing *don't look at me* to a prostitute

It's hard to miss the bone-
deep difficulty inscribed
within so-called *recreation*

*

The sidewalk hustlers in-
voke the fiscal year

*

Awash in a vast, poison
voice that needs—with the
force of a trillion dollars
and a million finer futures
foreclosed—to be heard,
how shall you live?

A woman carries the idea
of *a pretty girl* around her
like a cloud of pepper spray

*

Sometimes I think you
people actually like all this
cancer

*

The time fills on the landfill.
A shy-faced tourist con-
stantly nearly reveals her
breasts

There's no such thing as life, Mom, I hear from a passing phone conversation

*

Merchandise and biomass on the avenue splits like a zipper at the hobo negotiating a new covenant from the double yellow line

*

Every year, it gets harder to imagine words that will do more good than harm

We professionals live in the
shadow of nearly becoming
victims to the arrogance
we enjoy

*

Some blend of current,
crosswinds and customs
keeps the saint at sea

*

The tide is tired

The words show the
invisible: a modern office
building, a molten orifice
budding

*

Complexity creates de-
pendency. Beware vam-
pires in these parts

*

The horror of being
addicted to something
other than French fries and
happy talk

Heads up: The *real* in real estate doesn't refer to reality

*

Consensus is a desert. But you need to go to an actual desert to see that sometimes

*

The spectacle is a relief. Any story we can share is a refuge from our private burrows

The man who'll give you an
enemy implacable enough
to   protect   you   from
yourself is the best friend
you ever had

*

Head swapped in by thrifty
sculptors, eyes washed of
witness—the ever-troubled
prophet and the ever-
present chopper-off of the
prophet's head

*

But there is a certain mind
that forgets nothing and
forgives less. There is a
certain mind

Maybe we can't understand
ancient Egypt because we
can't understand our own
civilization

*

An opiate must be joyless
for it to be endemic

*

The shadows chuckle

I say *fuck it, I can live on my wits and $10 a day.* Then I'm getting lunch at a cart, and a scabby-faced guy comes up and says *you're a very rich man*

*

Time acts like money, piling up in vaults. Money acts like time, going away

*

Hurry past the reflective curtain wall of the momentarily profitable

Who can take re-
sponsibility for the sins and
abuses that birthed them?
Who can take re-
sponsibility for the fun-
ctions of their liver and
kidneys?

*

Session expired. Forty
more years of usernames
and passwords. Secrets
successfully modified. No
cost, except you want to
live a little less afterwards

There's a semi-visible monster under the streets and you can either die trying to face it or die trying to pretend it's not there

*

We'll email you a bill of rights

*

There's usually two or a hundred ways to do something that are easier than making it good

Sandwiched between the airplanes and plumbing in a leviathan's smile-frown, I feel less like a strident negotiator than the terms of someone else's settlement

*

The challenge with any bounty—of time, talent, money, or beauty—is how to best squander it with manifestation

*

Are the singers ripping themselves off? Is a tree ripping itself off when it puts forth a flower?

A laxative paradox, indeed.
But who can relax for long
enough to ponder it?

*

The omnipresent tyrant-
celebrity is the same but
different each week: a pre-
failed talisman against the
dark night of the soul

*

Try to shoehorn your talent
into the charred crust of
the world

To mass-produce yourself
and go to sleep seemed the
best way to cope with
eternity. Publishers and
cameras appeared—com-
mon and cheap as sand

*

The plane's wings are
always nipping the tree
branches

*

The craftsmen embellish
the surviving idols with the
skins and regalia of the
ones we just euthanized

There will always be ample hats and T-shirts for the people who can never belong to enough armies

*

Just when your expectations of the world reach their lowest, it's time to meet the unbounded expectations of your son. This crossing is the site of a miracle

*

Workaday days and nights are fine food for the photosynthesis of misprision

A wild oak grows tangent
to the tilt and thrust of
reality

*

Everyone agrees this is a
fallen world. But what it's
fallen from is baffling past
discussion

*

Reality's a feckin disaster, a
chaos of chapstick, tob-
acco and gum kisses,
followed by the acid
discharge of septicemic
feelings

Demoralized by contemp-
orary life? Try another
fucking compromise!

*

Everyone says the world is
unfair. Then one person
says *let's see just how*
unfair

*

The ashes of tomorrow
drift into our caviar

In a bird/angel language, my infant son describes the lake and river systems of the northeast

*

You never know who's gonna wanna settle a score with eternity

*

The dollars press to disproven release within an engine running on un-intended consequences. Safety is a hallucination based on wishing-well capital projections

It's no coincidence that something so shallow and dubiously alive as a virus should undo us

*

Then came the year we failed at all the shit we probably never should've been doing in the first place

*

Was it a field of stars or the coiled scales of a black serpent?

The first blossom bounces
silently on the subway's
linoleum floor

*

As the plague descends,
Sikh prayers whine from
the liquor-store TV

*

The Thing You Thought You
Saw—Yes, It Meant That

The city's theophany goes
occupying-army quiet

*

Throughout this reasonable
duration in the best of all
possible worlds, it's always
going to be a crisis, either A
La Carte or BYO

*

Everything, to a baby, is an
antique

No one's ready for now.
Never have been

*

A spiritual problem, turned
from the door, dresses as
an epidemic to get in—
Trojan horseplay at its
finest

*

There's no good outcome
for a balloon

Metaphors jump the blood-brain barrier and kill you just the same

*

Under permission of the synonym, asterism swaps for constellation, lips swap for a bear swaps for a spoon. The speaker begins to sense just what they're up against

*

Go to where it is unbearable. Go to where you're unbearable. That's all the exercise I'd recommend

Big earphones became respirators we had to wear to buy wine through plywood windows

*

Empty F trains gleam as they cross the Circumferential Parkway

*

Deferred costs come due in a foam of bankruptcies like the million fluttering eyelashes of the windy commuter train platform— on schedule

The moon repeats herself
in step with forgetfulness,
and makes a new moon

*

No one said the jubilee
would be so frightening

*

To die young in bank
marketing is hideous and
cruel

The resale price of the obvious never seems to benefit me

*

To hear of such a thing as a well-recorded 169,000-year astronomical cycle will leave a mark on you

*

It was a beautiful bummer—a time and place where being wrong was as easy as opening your mouth

Liars come in choirs

*

Putting nuts into shells is a
bad job

*

Washing the sugar off pills
is a bad job

Grinding rubble into sand is
a bad job

*

Either historical fiction or
it's science fiction: There
are no other genres for this
ridiculous year

*

Who can say what time it
is? Every savior makes it
their business model to
disagree

My compatriots flee with
enough food and soft-
faced idols to last the night

*

The river of wood spreads
through a continent of air
and vanishes into the
thirsty sky

*

Would you speak as if no
one's ever said a word?
Could you?

There's no place for your
unique identity in traffic

*

The wilderness of Abraham
is alive and well in the eyes
of strangers and the trees
at dusk

*

The act of washing dishes
is but a deeper kink in the
labyrinth that an exploding
star makes

Then I wake up one Tuesday, awash in the mercy of not being too late for anything

*

She looks like her dad, if he was as pretty as her mom

*

The marshals seized the storefront where my daughter pondered puppies

My daughter and I went out
by the sunflowers and the
parking lot to drink the air

*

Reality is playful, but so
hard to get to

*

Daddy, I make you special,
she says

Mere I am, she says, upon the sea. *Mere I am*, but never to me

*

A trillion atoms over a trillion years will only find their ways to sit side by side to watch this TV show one single time, unless there's a rerun

*

Take good care of that garbage truck

When your employer is a flesh-eating bacteria, hitting those deadlines will only get you so far

*

Tired of survival, people say quietly, if they say it at all

*

Go looking for a weather forecast and ten thousand ransom notes pour in

There's always work
digging subbasements un-
der whatever hell you're in

*

Grabbing at a hand from a
passing train—I never
guessed that would
become a fantasy of
stability. But here we are

*

A People's Oral History of
Easy-to-Watch TV: Every
day leaves us fragile and
unforgiving

We turn on each other,
almost always for some-
thing embarrassing

*

The word *unbearable*,
when spoken, is usually a lie

*

There will always be folks
who say it was better when
the lizard people ran things

What matters has perhaps always been an illusion. But when the illusion gets truly threadbare, TV critics claim the force of the four horsemen

*

The heart is no warm 60-watt incubator. It's a thresher. The heart... watch out!

*

There are rooms where no one can do anything quite right, where it's none-theless hard not to blame yourself

Scratches in a notebook
and creases under eyes in
an otherwise pretty face,
with tiny numbers beside
each line like a countdown
to Knowing Better

*

The birds and the bees are
frisky between bank-
ruptcies

*

When the angel reveals her
fullness, you'd be wise to
lower your chin and make a
fist

Turns out the people are the hoax. It'll blow over soon enough

*

Permission to be stupid, sir!

*

Baseball introduces the word *consecutive* to the boy, hinting at the silent triumphs of adulthood

Penmanship, sculpture and gift wrapping are only a few of the delicate acts from which I have recused myself

*

What gets you is the echo

*

A poor man's possessions multiply like fractions as they get fewer. The room-for-rent photo in the flyer will never be entirely free of debris

G-d talks to every thief. But only the best ones know not to listen for too long

*

Something matters here in the city. It's the ball under one of these three cups

*

Everyone wants something for nothing. So the smart folks invent new nothings of even less substance

I spent an entire, terrible, pointless, sleepless night trying to reset myself to a diamond

*

The puzzle doesn't fill in. It expands

*

Money, naturally, gets tired—almost as tired as it makes us

The money always gets tired before it can explode. But some people only ever want to explode

*

I heard about the butterfly wings that started a hurricane and said I'm gonna get me a thousand of them butterflies

*

My father calls and tells me he can no longer ascend a stepladder to change a lightbulb

Plan-B careers tend not to make sense. *So your problem isn't that you have to lie, but that you're not in charge of the lies?*

*

The bombers that streak above the joggers are just another charm on the afternoon's bracelet

*

We boys who traded in report cards for paychecks woke middle-aged, with lives bounded by pain we'd only describe as *going back to those rooms*

The brook's respectable
cousin is a canal

*

The music doesn't drone or
joke or malinger. It only
intensifies or speeds away

*

Maybe the TV listings had it
right, and the real triumph
is a mere *coming to terms*

The Boss can spot a malingerer, especially a talented one. You can outrun and outpunish him, but only for a while

*

The cash register behind your face isn't as natural as some folks like to say

*

Only years later did we learn about the terrible affliction suffered by the bullet that killed the president

The wall of disdain between innocent people and the people who sinned to buy their innocence is a load-bearing wall

*

They call him a rich man, but he's just expensive to be around

*

There's tension in a standing structure. A tower is a kind of bomb

Nothing works all the time.
And sometimes, nothing
works at all

*

No advice. Fuck advice

*

The tabletop trembled as
the trucks passed. The
landscape did more with
less

Natural and unnatural advantages mingle in the flying buttress of hips, portcullis of pelvis, aluminum shoulders and pigeon-proof eyebrows

*

You can hold out against the evidence of the senses, but only for so long

*

You need an ace in the hole that can survive the acid current of jokes you need to stay free

Every shadow starts in the sun

*

The sunny meadow of humanity revealed by a mandolin must also become a tomb, simply by dint of all the things it isn't

*

In the end, I'm pitting demons against demons to nurture something that has never existed

But when the demons
bubble down—what a foul
calm!

*

Small-town snow stains the
brown yellow slopes on a
string of sunny false-spring
days

*

Every liberation is also a
trap. Buck, laddy buck.
Buck!

They call it a business, but
it's a for-profit totalitarian
cult run by people who
know the secular never
really was

*

The television fixes me in
its blind primary-color eye
with a letter or number
inside and says I've been
communicated with

*

Nothing provokes quite like
an absence

One day, they will ask you to sign up to die. Only then will they break out the beauty

*

Some folks get their kicks swearing up and down that we're all sinners who spent all the money we never even had. I never got why they like to say things like that

*

You open the door, innocent, and step onto a sidewalk the color of cooked sausage

A weird poverty rises as material conditions im-prove

*

My path vanishes in the underbrush of potted plants killed by Frank Sinatra's martinis

*

The in-flight magazine explains an ancient metropolis like it's a familiar piece of software

Some folks own the copyright on the lie they told you, so you can't remind them of it

*

The executioner's tits are impeccable

*

Spring comes on with contradictory weather, like a liar's mix of apology and threat

Anyone can lash out, but who's damaged enough to sustain an assault?

*

I too am often too eager to take my cues from the worst that's been done to me

*

The library is a no-holds-barred streetfight for understanding and for joy

The first guy to run a marathon died young as a junkie, a little younger than an alcoholic. He died on the job

*

When you suspect that what you love is ultimately nothing, you start playing footsie with nothing's foxy cousin, death

*

The old men with strollers full of probably garbage and old women in sexy heels say: *When I'm dead, bury me. Until then, figure it out*

The tremendous ad-
vantage of a mistake is that
you've already made it

*

Speech and sex are higher
excrements, and the
cement of cities

*

Hooray for fun

There are afternoons when G-d seems to ask, with genuine interest: *How real would you like it to be?*

*

Original impulses recede. Kluges span the gaps. Bills come due. Cost eclipses vision. Altar for sale by owner

*

Rising prices are the paper of the news: the near-murder, the divorces and half-orphans, the promises people could only afford to make

What? Admit I'm a decaying bag of historically discredited meat with a third-rate education and no legitimate episteme-ological basis for speaking aloud? No thanks

*

Being one thousand dollars less fucked is worth being one million dollars more rich

Cargo in tall stacks drifts humbly from the meadow of the bay. Under the threat of distant, incredible violence, we arrange flowers

*

From the hand-curated, free-range nirvanas arises a new damnation: to be able to change how you feel with the caress of a sensor

*

The skies get so empty that a passenger jet sounds like a snowplow

Boats float on fog and the boardwalk fills with sand. Time and the ocean eventually make a lie of everything

*

To the everlasting shame of us talkers, the listeners outlast us

*

The past is a sibling conjoined to everything I see

Like divorced parents, the only thing the sun and moon have in common are us kids

*

A great sucking undertow pulls the plywood and paste from what we had for a golden age

*

I felt what I was for. I took a look at how I felt

What it's for is not how it
feels is not how it looks

*

Who changed the bedrock
of the human heart more—
Jesus or electricity?

*

In America when it is
America, the best and
worst live cheek by jowl

The only *gods* we openly adore—if we elect those terms—are the conspicuously shitty gods

*

Ambition is a risky way to understand

*

No one is as frenetic as a person dancing to a song that's ended

Pointless is the land.
Pointless is the child

*

There's an unseemly
slowness to the boardwalk
procession, like the tire
pressure had already
dispersed into the avenue
of death

*

Through the cracked plate-
glass window of the
kohanim room it's hard to
tell if the lights are on or if
the roof caved in

Judas, Judas, if you're able, keep your elbows off the table

*

Dip your nickel in the precious blood

*

Forty-three with a kiddo on my case, a second on the way, and a Gypsy curse on my sunglasses

Checks from the New York
Times and New York State
Unemployment.   Halfway
through   any   given
sentence I forget if I'm
bragging or begging for
help

*

Summer   rolls   up   the
crooked coast. Quarantine
curlicues of donut rubber
mark   the   intersections.
Wind rattles the roll-down
gates

In a stranger's downcast glance, you can see what it's like to nurse a sprained ankle in your soul for a whole life

*

People who speak of the *soul* are too often trying to win an argument they don't want to admit they're in

*

Alternating between science and blame, between early deaths and health regulations eschewed—I mumble in time with the moment

Grave marker and board-
walk, garbage fires in the
park and robot bones in
calzone alley. The calendar
doesn't care. No one cares.
Only you care

*

Alleyways swing past in
parallax, and for a moment
there's a clear way
through, a straight shot

*

The August afternoon gets
so hot that the words
November and *December*
sound phantasmagorical

The Spanish roof of the hilltop basilica passes for a school bus in the sky

*

Police, fire, sanitation, EMT—utility and symbol start to blend

*

How it looks is not what it's for is not how it feels

Pretty for strangers: Clean and simple, so they could draw your face with just two or three lines

*

The way we drink our time—it costs

*

Just because I have khakis on doesn't make me the politburo for an absurd reality

Summer nods its head. The whole earth sweats and begs for crime

*

Words aren't for that, is the reason in the overheard conversation, the song from the passing car. No shelter, no lesson—not in *words*, not for us, pal

*

Sudden delight of the sea in view! Old people past the breakers, past the bad habits of their genders, wading, arms bent and raised like wings that never materialized

We crowd the barricades
to become less than
ourselves, to become
material in a com-
prehensible design

*

Another soaring anthem
makes you complicit in a
scheme you otherwise
wouldn't touch

*

We don't only live, but
serve, like the half-sunk
barges and the fishermen
when you approach Coney
Island from behind

Our America was built on
jokes

*

Kelp-tangled   Neptune
bellows from a face upon a
tumbledown   amusement
warehouse. Whatever he's
bellowing, I bet it keeps the
world from collapsing

*

Ol' Zeus is a wilted fruit in
the summer sun. His open
shirt flaps farewell to the
passersby

It's so hot that the only way to move is to sit very still and let time handle the hauling

*

Mesopotamia translated through Scotland and an immigrant-stew house of horrors is a funny way to approach Jerusalem, a funny time to bring this up, a funny guy, but ain't we all?

*

A trillion screams tune each guitar string

Mired in drycleaners, liquor stores, bakeries—how shall such a layabout son of reality see?

*

What was the future? they'll ask. How we'll laugh!

*

The sky is full of minutes. But you can only get to them with your mouth

It feels so serious, but looks
so comical

*

He picks an asparagus from
the countertop and snaps it
open, looks inside. *Figures*,
he says

*

The end result was an
aerodynamic hobo with
digital tears—all the
options

Each year the dead get
more dead, until you round
an invisible corner and
start walking toward them

*

Death imposes its per-
snickety parallax death on
every event

*

Forms distort for a moment
and everything comes back
to everything, with a
fucking wink

The years melt homes and monuments   to   just moments

*

How it looks is not how it feels is not what it's for

*

The places we met were less than places. But we were never less than ourselves

I fumble to get my mask up
in time to tell people on the
street that they disgust me
and that I'm nobly saving
their lives

*

An artist? Or a salesman
rubbing a sick self against
the nation's health?

*

The prison and the shoals
of homeless are not
unintended consequences,
but an ancient and
ascendant point

I, too, often find myself taking the side of cruelty. I too often find myself taking the side of cruelty

*

Some folks will say that they're an accident, just so they can say you're one too

*

Feed the squirrels and you feed the rats reads the sign between luxury condo and riverine dump

Work distracts you from
mortality distracts you
from work

*

Private quibbles and ghoul
kibble—maybe   they're
poison. Maybe everyone is

*

Neither cruel nor vin-
dictive, she arrived early in
the place of adulthood,
with older boys—caterpillar
mustaches and varsity
jackets

Corsage for her wrist,
boutonniere for my jacket,
dancing, hands on waist or
shoulders, chaste but
touching, laughing, the
differences deepening be-
tween songs

                *

A thousand tricks buoyed
us from childhood to
parenthood—hairspray,
liquor, cigarettes, mouth-
wash, cheap thrills and
dirty jokes

A life doesn't extend like a line. It inflates evenly like a bubble. No matter the dimensions or duration, it is entire

*

Pimples dimpled the skin. Did the water ripple then?

*

I try to poke an antenna up between diaper changes, client calls, and con-versations with my wife that end with me saying *we'll work it out* over and over

I go into the woods at night with a flashlight and call most of the forest the unlit part. Talk to me about *the unconscious*

*

A life insurance nurse comes to the house to put my pimpled Irish ass on their spreadsheet—another pork belly on the exchange

*

The pressure transmutes an individual to a commodity, then to a sensation

The frontiers that kept us
sane are unreliable

*

Go ahead—argue with the
barber. See what that gets
you

*

We live in a residue,
perhaps as a residue,
cussing our luck and
plotting vengeance on
what has long since
forgotten us

Latex underwear and Cobra health insurance: the amenities of exile

*

Why's it gotta be so hard? has two working answers. 1.) *It just does.* 2.) *It doesn't.* Anything else is pure fuckery

*

We all got problems. Just ask the mailman's pod- iatrist's psychiatrist's nut- ritionist's mailman

The problem calls for professional agonizing. So I hope you have time. No one who bills by the hour is a true enemy of nonsense

*

What monuments do we build when we know we will have been wrong? Lazy ones

*

The light by which one sees does not itself see. So, you're free

Sauntering diagonal on horseback across the spine of night, the drunk asked us *Tienes mierda?* It probably meant *do you have the shit?* But we heard it as *do you have the fear?*

*

Reserve egress

*

Are you afraid? flips to the question *Are you still willing to exist?*

By the forty-second Armageddon you start to take the hint

*

Each step along the low, low road will feel as if it was your own idea. Perhaps that's a mercy

*

Deli shelves fill with MREs for the war on boredom and the war on yourself during a long, noisome summer when one war bleeds into the next

It's bedtime. I break a piece off of a child's toy to stir my drink

*

American cities burn on the news. I spend the afternoon with mismatched screws, building a crib

*

I stalk the ice cream truck up the fringe of the park. I argue with my daughter about bedtime, argue with my wife about whose turn it is to worry

Forty-three—I could've said
the thing, or caught the
bullet, or stopped the
bulldozer, or the bill.
Something. But I didn't

*

Those days wouldn't go
fast enough, but expired
with uncontrollable swift-
ness. I guess they're still like
that

*

People sprang into the
streets to protest the
police, to challenge the *use
of force*, as we called it
then

It seemed that beauty had obsolesced, even as a weapon

*

Any makeshift mercenary mistruth can become numinous when perceived by us who're numinous

*

I lost my job. I wrote books, and the slimy junk that paid. I took your sister on my bicycle in loops around the shuttered golf course

There were murders done in the name of law, order, skin and property. It was an awful abuse, and I hope you find it awful still

*

Your mother and I sweated and cursed the world, but never each other. We kept it close—a family grows into a cult of sorts

*

There's no survival without faith—in each other, in the future, and trailing behind is the ever-faltering faith in ourselves. We cleaned and cooked and worked

We did everything that was asked—but we had different voices asking us

*

I read Bible stories to your sister at night. She liked how *all the stories knew each other*, and I said, *yes, they knew us, too*

*

My Massachusetts accent unfurled at the mention of *G-d*. I preferred it to *lord*— an old revolutionary aversion to calling anyone, even the author of the universe, *lord*

Maybe it was those Manhattans, or just to keep her from interrupting, but I read those bedtime stories loud

*

It's a lot of work, getting the house ready for a baby. A lot of work for a dad, newly unemployed, with hopes unfulfilled and goofy. A lot of work for a mom, rightly worried

I had my schemes—a sitcom about a graveyard. Sorry about that. I lacked a nose for what people wanted, or I just didn't want such a nose

*

You'll see why, or maybe you won't—G-d knows what kind of dad I'll be to a son, and what that'll do to you

*

The wars call out like unanswered questions. On a breezy summer day, we eat chips by their memorials, confounding and fulfilling their hopes

Take the loophole, and then
loop home

*

Though we lived in view of
the LaGuardia, Newark and
JFK flightpaths, we saw
one or two airplanes a day

*

I try to say what I mean, but
all the words are peasant
verities or medieval kluges
or sound effects keep a
drowsy customer awake—a
thousand years past their
inspiration dates

Those plague days were
like a dream, little details
askew by a few degrees

*

It seemed everything was
about to change—explode,
perhaps—and for real this
time. But I'd felt that way
since I was sixteen. You'll
see, I hope

*

A baby is born. And now I'll
never truly be a stranger
again. Every ribbon ties,
every bow crosses its arms
and widens its eyes

Sunrise over the farthest
Rockaway jetty, and
Manhattan still a palace of
night—desolate and askew

*

Birth and death crowded
together unabashed in the
operating room. For a
moment, the reality of
being alive exceeded every
condition or purpose laid
upon it

I was a grownup then,
handling diapers and
automobiles, driving
through the longest tunnel
from the hospital to our
home in the shadow of the
biggest bridge

*

Such tunnels and such
bridges! New York rich
enough to regret the sea!

*

Regret foams like the edge
of a towering wave, shines
like the surge that
incinerates the filament

White light flares in the
bathroom. Blood slops on
the floor. New schemes
anchor and liberate the
almighty soul

*

Protestors in the park press
their advantage. The by-
standers hope it's simple
revenge. Into it all, comes a
baby

*

The baby looks around,
more hungry than
impressed

We test every surface. The diners dine until dined upon. Dancers dance until danced upon

*

The baby opens his eyes here and there to track the voices. He has no questions. It's all self-evident to the baby

*

A crescent moon hangs above the timid rest-auranteering of a pan-demic summer night full of inconsequential fireworks

We can be so many things,
under one single name

*

For daddy and baby alike,
the adventure looks like
squirming, mostly

*

The more moving parts, the
more that can go wrong.
We advance in step with
calamity

Every maelstrom of desire
matures into a quaint small
town

*

A voice from the sidewalk
calls out *salami*

*

I do not know. And yet, life
and death seem to hinge on
acting as though I do

Into it all comes a baby. It all comes into a baby

*

She handled the baby and I handled the road, while the baby handled something else—a job I know, and an important one, though I don't know its name

*

A crying child filibusters me from interminable debates. The ad for an exercise machine ceases to be a threat to my legendary sanity

I spend wordless days in
the gentle expectant
breathing of a watched
animal

*

There are a trillion dead
chickens in each practical
idea. But the outcome still
depends on the astro-
logical position of garbage
herders migrating toward
a rumor of six-cent
redemptions

*

At the middle of the
maelstrom, what's wrong
with the world becomes
what's right with it

Blue veins throb in a newborn's temple and a mother's breasts. At night, blue lightning flashes in the clouds

*

Price tag, shoe name, boat profile, hair style, minor skyline—the sun sings *it's all more to see, more to see*, and tramples the optic nerve

*

The capillaries of unending punishment flow through time, invisible until it's too late

The infant with a pacifier looks like Gabriel with his horn

*

I wonder how anyone imagined such a thing as open space or simple form, then I see the shock the first time a milkfed baby drinks cold water

*

Don't forget cherubs and spare ribs, bagel stores and dinosaurs

My little girl makes colorful
bookmarks for the books
she won't let me finish

*

A paper wall offers polite
isolation from an otherwise
deadly universe

*

You sketch to com-
memorate when the
subject best threatened sit
still, or just when it best
resembled something

With lights, cranes and
sound effects, men make
believe

*

The notebook goes in a
shopping bag, crumpled
with still more lines, each a
minuscule kick in the
gonads

*

Imperfection finds us—the
sooner the better

The only time the cat won a staring contest in its twenty-one years was right before it died

*

Summer's promontory is an old military concern sold as a tonic to the vainglorious work camps of the Eastern seaboard. All the streets end in ocean

*

Only later do we learn what the madman did with the brook and the beehive

For all our talk of dominion and damnation, the crickets don't seem to have noticed

*

The bears hide, but none are as depressed as the ones they hide from

*

Past the ice cream shop, shuttered for the evening, the ocean spreads upwards—another, lesser sky stacked up until morning

Tri-state dads are indistinguishable from one another on the beach. Bellies like bellows, they bark about saltwater

*

Tri-state wives save the box tops and cut the coupons of eroticism

*

Boat shoes and sandals for showered ankles in the early evenings when the dads realize *oh, it happened to me too*

Sometimes playing dumb is the smart move. Sometimes being dumb is the smart move

*

I say I'm a mountain, but I'm a sandbar, a barrier island. The hoteliers may shell out to shore it up another season, or they may not

*

Someone is dying. Someone eats their first arancini

Knowledge is a whirlpool. I can see its tightening bottom but can't imagine where it empties out. I can't imagine surviving the journey

*

A baby's spit-up bleaches the wine stain from an undershirt

*

To kick against the pricks is only cute when you're a rising prick

The docks are crowded
with wooden chests and
plastic coolers of words.
Some lads carry past a
shark cut lengthwise in
quarters

*

Every business is import-
export. We each make our
living in someone else's
subliminal

*

Reality has always been
largely unprofitable

Borders dissolve and the import-export business pivots to the obfuscation economy

*

Every shark feels a sensation adjacent to pain when the fin emerges from the water

*

Nightmares made of nightmares construct a nightmare—a mire of spittle wire, a tangle in Medusa's hair on a humid night, a home

The shark may have been a killer, but he was always nice to me

*

I waste hours trying to see what I saw, to feel what I feel, to say what I feel

*

Clouds travel over our dinner. Broken storm bones seek another storm in which to fuse and to break

A clue to life on other worlds appears from the blood in the breastmilk and the first diaper after the circumcision

*

It's so insane what makes up the best days of our lives

*

My baby boy kicks his own wounded penis. It's a nightmare, a dream come true

The scream teases a new
note into the afternoon

*

The joy of a child's birth
isn't simple. In it lies the joy
of agreeing to perish

*

Rain pastes leaves to a
funeral home's awning.
Wind comes next, but
when?

The last young man outside the Eden Farms minimart to put his shirt on will necessarily believe himself possessed of a special destiny

*

Mourners and new parents keep equally odd hours

*

I hold the crown of your head under mine like a violin. The plates of your skull expand, finding the seams along which they'll seal

Halos of alluvial sand shoal
the landing gears of reefers
parked a year in front of
the storefront funeral home

*

I stay up late with you and
sing a lot—mostly about
milk and the virtues of
going back to sleep

*

Cold weather found me—
breast milk in my thin hair
and talk of pony crimes on
my lips—yawning with awe,
yawing with awe

The balloon's pop brings
the hard truth of time close
enough to kiss. The child's
whole body rebels against
it, tries to dry-heave it
away

*

The baby gives a look that
says: *I am the entire
universe and you are
messing with me*

*

It was a golden age of
walking into walls. Key
rings filled the streets.
Strangers left them on
standpipes, top bolts of
hydrants and base ridges
of lampposts

Summer poaches the
clouds like eggs. The moon
is a melting pat of butter

*

A billion blushing angels
color each red brick. What
a thing—to walk down the
street!

*

Bush-league suns peek
from the folds of a garbage
dump

Archons and guardian angels, aliens and ghosts, Frankenstein and Christ revived are not creations, but holes punched in a dark box, like they said stars were

*

Wadded-up week-old pleas from the canned goods aisle make the fire purr tonight

Gingerly walking my infant son down the narrow hallway back to his crib, I feel the eyes of my ancestors upon me. In his bedroom, the baby monitor chirps with feedback

*

Pain is the port. The vast ambiguous galaxy of joy is the storm

*

Fifty cents of butterfly wheezes, a billion dollars of sunlight—mind-altering substances abound

More Adventures of a Likeable Character: The creative guy cooks nice dinners, makes up games with his daughter, surprises his wife. That's all

*

There are afternoons when G-d seems to ask, with genuine interest: *How easy do you want things to be?*

*

Ten years married, I still smell my shirt before putting it on

Doing your best—especially if you fail—is an act of respect toward what matters and an act of hope for those to come

*

Dreams presume to say what your life means. Then you presume to say what it means. It's a jig around the treacherous flame

*

I balance on the seam where accidents stop happening and where they start again

Save whatever you have to.
But don't save the world

*

This Tiresias has radial tires
for eyes

*

Blind force would bury
even the memory of sight
beneath the flat flesh of the
brow

No one can keep the day of their death from being referred to as a Wednesday, or a Thursday, one of those fuckers

*

A voice flashing silver and orange says *good luck with your poetry*

*

I had to blind myself to nuance to stay kind

Swaddled in diagonal stripes, head askew in the direction of a dropped pacifier, my boy is the image of a whirlwind falling carelessly asleep

*

My son. I see you new, and yet yoked under a curse adjacent to my own

*

Only G-d can pick up Daddy

Someone catches you looking into their blood. A ripple runs through them

*

No one can teach you what you actually need to know—how to be hit in the face and have it not matter

*

The question of my father must remain open in order to hold ajar the question of myself

A Juniors cheesecake for
our wedding anniversary,
and so our daughter can
end her day with
something sweet

*

A jagged poignancy snares
the lightning strike

*

Do not underestimate the
degree to which your
freedom is someone else's
opportunity

The plane's rear hatch opens onto a sled trail down to a foamy sea. As you glide to the beach, the crowd cheers

*

I invoke the right not to find out until it's too late

*

The messages in bottles bobbed back to shore. It was the ocean, asking if we planned to give back all that wind

Saying that *everything is just fine* is a weapon sometimes

*

The test in middle age is to be buried alive and not complain

*

The only one who will tell you anything is free is a salesman

A woman seems assembled
from frontiers and coast-
lines. A man seems a lazy
gonad in a complicated
splendor

*

The hope in which I act is
tea-stained the color of
people recklessly sainted
by the daguerreotype—
brown bruises in pale fat

*

Free reads the pink post-it
on the oversize can of
peaches in the crook of the
old woman's arm

Rain rain rain—even the sun
is rain. Time is rain. It's a
rainy night. Come to the
city. See the great plans,
cooked in rain

*

I asked the trees *How can
you go on, baiting an
implacable force?* They
answered with one voice
*One day, we're going to
strangle that bastard sun*

*

Confusers *would* hide their
tons of gold under Liberty
Street

There is no smooth, dry
side of a junkie upon which
to adhere the logo decal

*

Freedom   expensively
bought isn't much freedom
at all

*

I'm lucky no one listens
when I claim responsibility
for the traffic, the rain and
the curse

Freedom, like the Camaro, is a promise we can only muster the energy and the stupidity to believe for a short while

*

Older than rock n' roll or Dionysos: To deliver your species' most vital truths, and eschew survival. What a spiritual discipline! Who wouldn't want to hear the results!

*

Another health, another death

Sadists and masochists take turns on a single wheel, weathered beyond tread

*

You never know where the last straw will find you

*

The breakdowns at an awards ceremony are split equally among winners and losers—not much among the staff, busy plating cakes and touching up cracks in the plastic crowns

Citizens and customers
behave differently, see
differently, matter
differently and die
differently

*

It's the kind of night when
everyone accuses every-
one else of being a movie
star in the Reade Street
Pub. My motives are as
obscure as theirs

*

Just ask an unscrubbed
summer-school bully, and
he'd tell you if he could:
Neurosis is the best way to
control something smarter
than you

Standing at the door of the train, a woman leans back to welcome the morning rush. Static electricity draws a few strands of her long hair to my short-cut crown

*

Death is vanishingly difficult

*

Good luck to us spawn and apostles of The Promised Cardiac Arrest

How do people deal with the certainty of death? Some better than others

*

A personality is an unstable combination of how it looks and how it feels. By the time it appears, it's too late to ask if it's voluntary, or what it's for

*

Like Odysseus weeping bitterly one four-star morning-after with Calypso: It's not what he wanted, but he sure did stay a while

Rage is a reliable holiday
from doubt

*

Your hat says something
that your plastic shopping
bag disputes

*

Pretending sanity, I swore
my enemies were outside
myself

You call him president. I call him a man who's found his foolhardy way into the very belly of a whale. And whales have no president

*

The professionals inflame an ancient hurt. You see a salesman do it, and you start to despise the artist

*

No president has ever been adequate to explain why I'm an asshole, or why you are

Free free free—for another five minutes—promises the bus carcass and busted water tower

*

The trench-deep gutter of autobiography—*I sold my soul for a pack of gum cause of the sorry place I'm from*—is what some folks expect when you flinch

*

I picked a side and got boxed in as bad as the last asshole. My aspirations became excuses, because I let everyone down. No, I did

Stay positive. Eat around the mouse's tail in the popsicle

*

You're only strong enough to kill me, and that's all you'll ever be

*

New York City in those days had the atmosphere of a cordoned-off escape

Absolute   father—the
weight of his gut rounds his
shoulders down and in—
ready to slip into reality
and never be heard from
again

*

They buried him before
things could get any worse

*

To the celebrity on the
sidewalk: *I go to reality to
get away from you people*

Those are the good guys?
I'll see you folks later

*

Young man full of sun/Old
man   crammed   with
vouchers

*

Rare is the progress not
reeking of ambush

I used to strut the library.
But one day, I noticed I
couldn't hold more than
seven digits in my mind at
a time. It was scary. It was
a reason to forgive

*

The only way to tell the
story of your job so
someone will listen is to
couch it as flattery or make
it a prelude to payment

*

The harbor smells of the
ocean one day and an
unventilated toilet the next.
How can anyone honestly
claim to love anything?

Angels taunt the clouds and the saints who see them into existence

*

In the realm of delight, if you're not ruthless, you're not credible

*

The lesson from tonight's beggar: *Don't laminate your pain*

So much of the day comes down to finding the thoughts that'll open or close the doors to dreaming

*

Monopile donut fender; sprinkler system synopsis; poor people with expensive strollers—each small thing changes the meaning of life

*

The clouds part for the Jehovah-cliche sunbeam to show you just where in Jersey to dig

Can of beer, Camaro gearbox and the hand that could be counted on to hit—you just want something that has something to do with you

*

Desire begins everywhere, supersedes itself ceaselessly

*

Pissed off, coiled like a walnut or flaring like a hoop from the surface of the sun: serpents always crushed, always whisper

Then there's another
body—arguments insinu-
ated in garments—another
urge, another bureaucracy
of fantasy

*

I conjure so much
browbent focus because I
can't even hold onto
unhappiness

*

A tide buzzes the bees,
blossoms the buds and
varnishes the veri-
similitude. But my foot still
grips the sand sometimes

When things get too
woolly-pully, honesty is
accidental, marked by
malapropisms and un-
intended meanings

*

Though warned, you wore
your nice shirt into the
brambles of time's own
fruiting and decaying
monsters

*

The mirror I call untrue
even as I negotiate with it—
it does hold my attention

He didn't want her more than anything—just more than he wanted to think his own thoughts

*

What's universal is often attended by some cautionary stink

*

The love songs on the jukebox can be sung addressed to G-d, then sung as G-d, then back again

When you feed the body to the mind, certain illnesses are inevitable

*

I've got to keep this guy happy. And as you can probably tell, that's no mean feat

*

The true crest of the city is a bright purple lipstick mark on a black plastic coffee-cup lid on a public bench outside the Salvation Army

Personal tastes being what they are, few are attractive to everyone. But even fewer are unattractive to no one

*

Ears like oyster shells: Yaquina little, Shigoku big. The line from chin to earlobe shows the way

*

Silence is an egg squeezed between warm knees. Water splashes. Every edge warms with negotiation. There is no calm solution

How it feels is not how it looks is not what it's for

*

When fantasies lose their perversity, beware of collapse

*

The body alone in the bar— was it pretty or merely appropriate?

A flowering father commits
his tulip atrocities

*

At sunrise, birds accuse
each other of having
trespassed into the timed
treasure vault of existence

*

You never want to see
inside of someone's body.
The problem is that
sometimes you think you
do

Wound up, alright. But like
a watch? Or like an apple
stem?

*

The game consists of
nearly missing a careless
woman's womb

*

But one day, winning feels
like busting up a junkyard

Bumps on a hastily shaven pudenda and an asshole like a shiny penny. Good luck to you if you call it lucky

*

Nothing is anything until it's too much

*

Sometimes   solace   is disgusting

Secret thoughts on
awnings and marquees
accuse me of my next
treachery

*

Clothed in sleepy clitoral
hoods of resentment until
stirred to destructive
frenzy, we wait our turn to
dare a void of sprain

*

Tell it terrible

The galaxies beyond our
grasping metaphors in-
spire bitter vengeance: the
sciences, creative arts and
so-called wonder

*

The pain of wanting bleeds
into hatred of what you
want

*

What a strange, strange
war the men and women in
the city have dressed for!

Desire negates its pro-
fessor, as its objects
expand

*

Hills and valleys of some
odd topography pull on
every object

*

One night, my body was
disheveled to a tangle of
snakes, and every question
of eating or standing or
breathing was thrown open

A land without depressions
is just a map

                    *

Hunger   never   becomes
responsible

                    *

Some folks despise every
truth, law and opinion,
except the voice that says
*Yes, you deserve more
pornography*

From the angel-avalanche
above the church door; the
insignia that spans public
and intimate sections of a
woman's   thigh;   the
interlocking *H*s of the
parking   lot,   another
literacy beckons

*

With toothsome, handsome
faces, corralled celebrities
dress the global-industrial-
informational billions up as
a village

*

Some questions lead you to
a butt plug with an eye that
slowly opens and closes

Desire flickers out like the lights, revealing a land-scape devoid of intrinsic value, and, hopefully, something else

*

Some folks say the trees are going out of business

*

Everyone is a substitute for someone else, back through the service entrance of biography to the beginning of time. Tracing it all back wouldn't be worth it is the sense I get

Vengeance fills in the details of the final object of desire

*

If I don't exist, then why am I only hearing about it now?

*

The addicts form a circle beside the obelisk, in the shadow of the cannon

A promise hollers to be
remembered in the current
of druthers, ruby cabernet
and amber rye, the
wedding ring diluted in a
dozen other rings, in
ancient Jerusalem, late for
a plane

*

A little oblivion can be
salutary

*

Our bodies are not
obscene. But their de-
mands on one another, and
on ourselves, often are

Beach nipples stare out—
vicious brown anemone
mouths

*

I rise on arms like towers of
skulls and thrust into a
tunnel of blindness that
necessarily narrows

*

Why'd you do those things?
Now replace *pressure* with
pleasure, then try it the
other way

What you would call a
failure of love is in fact its
survival

*

Making love in the light of
an alarm clock and a baby
monitor, a bruise shifts its
countenance

*

A lot of what some folks call
truth is just where guesses
tend to gutter out

In lucid or blessed moments, what comes from us seems instead to come to us. The wind spins the fan blade. The heat abates

*

The face is still there. But below, the legs walk a pianola treadmill

*

Believe, the singer says, *that you have just about all the time in the world*

The shortcuts through the pun and the notorious number are untrustworthy, but ancient

*

Every year there were more dinosaurs in the Bible

*

Music makes fugitives of us—a gull on the wing one day, clinging like barnacle the next

That the tequila shot stays
down she marks with a nod:
A victory and an assent to
all that comes next, even if
it's only another drink

*

You'll never impress G-d
with your perfection

*

The bar accurately reflects
our status as fallen
creatures

The bridge devoured forty
city blocks to get so high.
Heed the cost, for the cost
heeds not you

*

Strange voices cluster
around mundane objects,
insisting that we look
elsewhere

*

If you want cheap,
comfortable pants, then
you must be comfortable
with what it took to get
them to you so cheaply,
and with what you'll
overlook to be comfortable

I order one more glass of whatever will make me feel like a fact in a world of rumor

*

The final prayer is not for a vision of adamantine completeness to shatter the skulls of porridge-indifferent peers, but for a clue to console my ultimate failure

*

I am drunk enough to know that I'm not drunk enough

It's one of those afternoons when you'd burn down the city to buy some time. But where will you spend the time? And don't say another city

*

There are immoral obligations in a glass of tap water, and the escalator demands blood. Spandrels of cowardice drown us scoundrels

*

The expenditure required to clean a place and make it worth cleaning is the stuff of saintly faith and devotion

Being alive is an untenable position, exacerbated by the insane stakes of selfhood. It's enough to make a person cautious

*

He was trapped by time, remorse, desire, disgrace, and some gossamer thread of success. Sound familiar?

*

The North American continent is littered with landscapes humming *this is still okay* to a tune that has stopped playing

Welts and songs notwith-
standing, Ultimate Reality
takes the opportunities it
finds

*

I'm a cautious, clever
fellow. If I were to be
honest, what would that
even sound like?

*

Error is the signature

The men gathered to investigate reality and the intentions of its Author, using a billion-dollar sports team. They put some money on the outcome, just to make it interesting

*

UFO lily pads never quite touch reality and never quite escape

*

A wine cork and a cigarette filter stained with lipstick crowd the cobbles. Washington Square surges between the misspelled word and the word spilled right

What will you wear on your visit to the parts of your mind over which you have little say?

*

A billion perfections violently collide to make this thing

*

I drink because I may yet slur into accuracy

If you can, be careful where you go. Some places keep a corner of you forever

*

The left eye of G-d bores a hole in the bend of my brow to unearth the moment I yelled at the dog and the addict in the park

*

The karmic spindle of the American Northeast calls us to spin and be twisted

Go crazy enough for long
enough, and you get an ear
for what mental health
actually sounds like

*

I wouldn't trade it for all the
grenadine on Fort Hamilton
army base

*

Mothers and fathers tested
each other with tales of the
comedown room at the
Worcester Centrum

Warm air from the gulf—a
nice night to read ransom
notes

*

I wouldn't trade it for all of
Orson Welles' rubber noses

*

Gentle moments embroil
me in a billion-year
conspiracy of happiness

One day you will grow
strong enough that you can
afford to remember what
was done to you

*

The wicker headboard is a
veil over all possibilities,
like the surface of the sea.
Beyond it waits something
that justifies concealment

*

Each granted wish ups the
ante

This banter is a scheme of domestication exported to the ghosts and the gods by middle managers of the soul

*

He stopped talking about the drugs. But there was big hole where his life should have been

*

The mind runs rings around the heart, but can't leave it behind

Maybe love is just enemies-
against-enemies in a heist
of darkest night. But who's
to say we don't fall in love?

*

Hometown alchemy trans-
mutes what you hate most
into the dearest part of
your life

*

The lace of the veil employs
every mystery—that we
may flit from miscon-
ception to misconception
until we properly conceive

Butchers and cops are kind
to one another

*

Pigeons swim the inter-
section above the
jurisdiction of the trash
can—testing time, wind,
leaves and the wariness on
every face. It's all a test, all
a result

*

Every face is a holy
question poorly phrased

How would outer space help? asks every book about outer space

*

To call life a part of something larger seems like a stalling tactic

*

Engine and radio on, the passing forms form a metaphor for what they are

Always the glass, for seeing
and for safety

*

Invisibility is one more
thread in the mask

*

Distance insists on a space
to sell or seduce ourselves
back into

I spend my days conceding
candy-colored   promises
and barking imperatives:
Go; stop; eat; sleep

*

Pain addicts and rubber-
neckers buzz like moths
around the darkest bulbs

*

Aliens, ghosts and the
internet—those final rail-
ings of comprehension—
seem   to   be   saying
something at first, but only
say what we think we want
to hear

You and I cut a swath
through more than just
time and space

*

People have apologized for
me. I never counted them
as doing me a favor

*

They caught the fat man
licking gizzards in a state of
gustatory sin, his epiglottis
all untucked

Past and future loop like cursive little bows to and from each of the invisibly small knots that we, in exasperation, call the present

*

What it's for is not how it looks is not how it feels

*

You complain that sympathy corrupts. We, the corrupt, can sympathize

Every new number is one
color gone

                    *

The avian muscles of a
woman's back and the
straining pilasters in an
ocean wave are palliatives
to interpretation

                    *

Illiterate predators effort-
lessly track me through a
wilderness of symbol

Atheist Jehovas and spherical Molochs grow confident that final comprehension is near. The planet closes in like an unhappy home

*

Sometimes a gentle, interesting thing delivers us from the world

*

We said we agreed to disagree. But I don't think we did

The cessation of inquiry,
even from honest ex-
haustion, is the death of a
man, the death of the sun.
Or it's the birth of a face

*

This holiday season,
remember: The sociopathic
institutions who kick
people out of their homes
are the only ones who can
feed the homeless

*

This holiday season,
remember: The companies
who steal you away from
your family all year can
help you win their affection

This holiday season, remember: With each passing winter, the price of survival gets more con-voluted, but never lower

*

Don't ever kiss the hologram. But don't ever let it see you refuse

*

The fruit of an evening's shamanic foray: *They did something terrible to us, and now we're their responsibility*

The kink in the crooked timber of humanity is a chore slipping perennially down the cosmic to-do list

*

You could play it straight. It isn't straight, though, is it?

*

The wonderful, terrible thing happened to me

Winning isn't like you think:
Each resident of the
dungeon is a dull ache of
despair for the king

*

Mushroom-cloud water
towers dot the postwar
suburbs of Long Island

*

Oh to be a man as free as
the markets are supposed
to be!

The train-facing graffiti ads and murals blur to *WHOWILLSTEALFROMYOU ANDHOW*

*

Oh to be as scary and wonderful as the worst curse word!

*

My body is collateral I wash and feed, left behind on a promise

So you flee to the traffic,
the great middle-distance
gaze of the earth—
assembled for something
else, going somewhere
else, the embodiment of
else itself

*

The face of the Holy Mother
surfaces from the center of
Taylor Ham to announce
there's more to us than our
nutritional value or our
price, even on special

*

The inmates started a
terrible fire

I get the feeling that I'm up against someone who is wiser than me, but who is not to be trusted

*

Language is so specific because the bulk of it tends to emanate from the least free people in each generation

*

In the commercial, the only onscreen obscenity is committed against *perfectly good cold cuts*. But the implications are explicit

In this do-it-yourself
country, people mostly do
things to themselves

*

The world doesn't end, but
ebbs into inefficient habits
of speech

*

I have seen love bend the
lawyers' language to
hieroglyphics, and I've seen
time turn a best friend to
unreliable rapping on a
seance table

289

How good some songs sound on a cheap plastic radio!

*

The shoplifter checks his haul of devices, designer water bottles, headphones, wallets, belts, peeling off labels. Over a train ride, everyone becomes an accomplice

*

Is there anything more intangible than the word *tangible*?

Money's finite. Intelligence's finite. Nerve's finite. Charm's finite. And every night when you go outside you see what's not

*

An unwelcome wisdom greets the question *Why would such a wise man lie to us?*

*

The mental illness sprung from the ruins of Coney Island may yet save us sinners in the hands of an angry network of sinners in an angry network

Better uses for us in the coming year!

*

Troubles pile up when you try stay inside an institution that can't manage, or doesn't remember, to be an institution

*

We are still here. We know what miracles feel like, and we don't care the cost. So, don't lose faith. We've never lost faith in you

Daddy wins the trophy of G-d and then he gets stepped on

*

Maybe honest men and women aren't honest because they're too dumb to lie! Impossible!

*

If a sin is a debt owed to G-d, and a debt binds two parties, then don't be too eager for forgiveness or too fastidious in your atonement

I couldn't stand around anymore with the ten million silent-film stars waiting for their luck to change back

*

Infinite power is for fools. To be alive is to maneuver amid innumerable limit- ations. It's as trivial as a dance. But what a partner!

*

The holiday cinches the hose. But the pressure presses. In my girl's tiny mouth, *Jingle Bells* be- comes *single G-d*

Where I Find the Time:
Every day's a jigsaw puzzle
while someone bangs on
the door. Absolute fucking
freedom for twenty-two
minutes, if you keep it
quiet—deal?

*

Within the tradition of the
skeleton, warpaths and
peacepaths mark the jowls
and the flaring temple arcs
from a million squints

*

They keep a lot of gravity
there. It's mostly imported,
and expensive

A lovely tattoo marked out
for the tumor the place to
make its home

*

Why not toss one more
dictat atop the creaky
tower of automaticity with
which you greet the minute
and the month?

*

The mind is the itch that
believes it's a scratch

Santa Claus disintegrates into geometric forms, but you never escape his charming gaze

*

Ashamed to mention the times when we didn't expect the burly earth to be ripped from under our blue suede shoes, we search out the rally point from the last failed assault

*

Forever's not my problem, except for about five minutes a day. It's a manageable devotion

I narrow down the riddle a little, while carnivorous plants crowd the front yard

*

At the bar, beneath century-old turkey wishbones whose owners never returned from the trenches, in a moment between the empty stein and the bill, we speak the word *progress*

*

It'll be unbearable around three in the afternoon. And it'll still be unbearable after a dozen dozen satoris

The screens are muzzles for my eyes. Then visible reality is a muzzle for my eyes. Then I come to a place where my eyes are muzzles

*

Among the handlers of Pan, there are paperback books that do something even if no one reads them

*

In the afternoon at the last tangle of wires before the bay, men hose down the not-for-hire oil trucks— forest green and emergency red

Under the expressway spur, my son's eyes darken to a supernatural blue

*

The city is symmetrical. If you miss anything on the way in, you can get it on the way out

*

A time is just a place you can't return to

Some of these days are hard, and I can't explain why

*

The highways are bad, but the distances are worse

*

The problem was the size of the miracles. I needed a truly miniscule miracle to get the gist of how a miracle might work

The land blisters with seers.
The vision is as sensible as
the details of a car going
60 MPH past my nose,
sensible as the fronds and
ribbons of a car wreck

*

Complaining we have to
live, complaining we have
to die, who can bear
creatures so tiresome as
we?

*

Knowledge was a stage like
adolescence, and no less
painful

The killing may be done by the sick. But the sickness was inflicted by the healthy

*

Just think what it'll be like to die, my little french fry

*

We can meet by the goiter in the interstate. Don't be late, unless you're late

Another time, per-
pendicular to time, extends
from its flat plane

*

Why is hate still holy?

*

Tomorrow you'll think
something totally different.
But this will still be true

Maybe I spent too much
time where lives work and
wives lurk

*

Maybe I knew that I'd walk
from this fire, into an
incredible darkness

*

Maybe I wasn't such a fool
as I needed to be

So far, my shabby understanding has done so much less harm than it could have

*

I am not a cosmos. I can go outside and get a cup of coffee

*

At the end the day will break. And you'll see you haven't made a single mistake

The baby will go on to say
something   altogether
different

*

One truth doesn't need to
know another truth to be
true

Forget This Good Thing I Just Said - About the App

What's going on? What do you need to hear? How can you move forward?

Finding an answer may be as simple as <u>swiping left or right.</u>

Forget This Good Thing I Just Said is a new experience, based on an old kind of book – the collection of short sayings, or aphorisms. By combining several hundred original aphorisms with the ring-oscillator software used in random-number-generating technology, *Forget This Good Thing I Just Said* offers up a completely unique experience every time you open it.

It's something literary, philosophical, and a little magical to brighten up your screens.

Find out more at:
forgetthisgoodthing.com

OTHER WORKS BY COLIN DODDS

Novels
Ms. Never
WINDFALL
WATERSHED
Another Broken Wizard
The Last Bad Job
What Smiled at Him
Vice Nimrod, Communications

Poetry
Heaven Unbuilt
Spokes of an Uneven Wheel
The Last Man on the Moon
The Blue Blueprint

Screenplays
The Sixth Finger of Tommy the Goose
But Let's Not Talk About Work
Climbing and Digging
Refreshment

About the Aphorist

Colin Dodds grew up in Massachusetts and lived in California briefly, before finishing his education in New York City. In addition to his books, his writing has appeared in more than three hundred publications, and been praised by luminaries including David Berman and Norman Mailer. He has also written and directed short films, and once built a twelve-foot-high pyramid out of PVC pipe, plywood and zip ties. He lives in New York City with his wife and children. You can find more of his work at thecolindodds.com.